Dear re

Thank you for buying this book, and more importantly, thank you for reading it. I hope that, in some small way, it will influence how you see, understand and carry out your work.

I'm deeply passionate about helping teachers improve, and am eager for Memorable Teaching to be a useful contribution to the profession.

If you have suggestions for how this book can be improved, be it a challenge to my arguments or an apostrophe gone awry, please do get in touch. I'd genuinely love to hear from you.

Peps
pepsmccrea@gmail.com

Memorable Teaching: leveraging memory to build deep and durable learning in the classroom.

Copyright © 2019 Peps Mccrea
Version 1.2, released January 2018
ISBN 978 1 912906 69 7

To Maimie, Mullen and all you other visionaries out there.

Contents

Preliminaries

Principles

About Peps

Peps Mccrea is an award-winning teacher educator, designer and author.

He is Dean of Learning Design at Ambition Institute, author of the High Impact Teaching series, and holds fellowships from the Young Academy and University of Brighton.

Peps has three Masters degrees, two lovely kids, and dances like no-one is watching (which is probably for the best)

Visit **pepsmccrea.com** for the full shebang.

Why memory?

*"Without an understanding of human cognitive
architecture, instruction is blind."*
Sweller

Memory underpins learning. Why then, as a
profession of *learning enablers*, it is something we
spend so little time talking about[1]?

Part of the reason is memory's historically *bad
reputation* in education circles. For many years it
has been associated with out-of-favor practices like
rote learning and *drill & kill*[2], and framed as the enemy
of rich and humane learning.

As a result, we have neglected to build a robust
understanding and common language around
memory, leaving us with an impoverished view of
its capacity, and a naive appreciation of the role it
plays in our classrooms.

For a profession so entangled with learning, this is a bizarre situation. However, it *is* beginning to change.

The rise of memory science

Over the last decade or so we've seen an increasing amount of memory literature published in accessible forms[3].

This, combined with the efforts of the 'evidence-informed' movement[4], has created a situation where many of the ideas presented within this body of work are increasingly finding their way into schools and classrooms around the UK and beyond.

Some of the ideas being explored are obvious. Others are deeply counter-intuitive. All have the potential to shine a light on our practice and nudge us to reflect on the reasons we teach like we do.

We stand to gain a great deal from these insights. Some of them are arguably the lowest hanging fruits of our current educational era. However, although their promise is encouraging, their form may not yet be sufficient.

The complexity of our craft demands coherent frameworks, organized around the decisions of our everyday practice[5]. Frameworks that make sense to teachers of all experience levels, and can be applied flexibly to meet the needs of a diverse range of contexts.

In short, we need scalable models for practice[6]. Which is exactly what Memorable Teaching has been written to do.

Why memorable teaching?

This book is the result of the lessons I've learned as a teacher educator, by helping hundreds of teachers to understand their practice and raise their game.

It is an attempt to stitch together the *best available evidence* around memory and learning into a coherent set of *actionable principles* that we can leverage to improve both our understanding of and impact in the classroom.

It is not a book about rote memorization or mnemonic tricks, or about turning you and your students into lifeless automatons.

It is about building deep, powerful and lasting understanding, by making your students more confident and independent, by making *you* more informed and effective.

Moving forward

As with most books, the more you put in the more you will get out. This book is a case in the extreme. Without action you will experience little change.

To help with this I've tried to keep my writing concise, and resisted including too many examples. Where examples *are* included, they tend to sit within a math(s) teaching context (my specialist subject).

I recognize that it would be better to have examples that are relevant to a greater range of contexts, but I have yet to find a way to do this with concision.

I have also signposted opportunities for further readings at relevant points so you can dig deeper into the areas that capture your interest.

The main chapters of this book are organized around *9 principles of Memorable Teaching*. To ensure these land with maximum impact, we first need to establish some fundamental assumptions around memory: its main components and how they interact.

And so that's where we're headed next. Strap in, it's time for a rough and ready tour of the architecture of memory.

Notes & further reading

1. For more, see *Visible Learning and the Science of How We Learn* by Hattie (p.162)
2. Joe Kirby argues that drill can thrill https://goo.gl/9Ch9uW
3. *Why Don't Students Like School?* by Willingham, *Visible Learning and the Science of How We Learn* by Hattie & Yates, *Make It Stick* by Brown *et al.*, *What Every Teacher Needs to Know about Psychology* by Didau & Rose, *The Science of Learning* by Deans for Impact, and *The Learning Scientists* blog are all stunning examples of accessible and rigorous writing around the science of learning and memory
4. If you get the opportunity, find your way to a ResearchEd.org.uk conference
5. For more, see *Building a Common Core for Learning to Teach* by Ball & Forzani
6. As Coe cogently argues in the foreword of *What Every Teacher Needs to Know About Psychology* by Didau & Rose

Memory architecture

*"If we don't understand something, we can't control it.
If we don't control it, we can't improve it."*
Harrington

From an educational perspective, the most useful way to think about memory is as a system of two interacting components[1]: *Long-Term Memory* (LTM) and *Working Memory* (WM).

Together, these components are responsible for pretty much all of the intended learning that happens in our classrooms. As such, it's worth taking some time to understand how they operate.

Our long term memory is our *mental model of the world*. It's a bit like a map. A map we construct ourselves, and use to help us make sense of and navigate our environment[2].

It represents what we know and who we are, and informs how we act.

Our LTM is composed of beliefs, understandings, mindsets, skills, dispositions, and facts. Although these things may *feel* quite different, for the purposes of this book we're going to think of them simply as different flavors of knowledge.

This knowledge is not static. It is constantly evolving and decaying as a result of our thinking and interaction with the environment. Our LTM is more like a forest than a library.

Powerful LTM

Life is an ongoing effort to upgrade our models of the world in an effort to make them more *powerful*. More powerful models mean more successful action. More successful action leads to better chances in life. This is what learning is and why schools exist.

Our job as teachers is to increase the life chances of our students by helping them develop more powerful LTM.

The power of our LTM is a function of two factors:

1. **Depth** How well *structured* our knowledge is. The more comprehensive and organized our LTM is, the better it performs for us in our lives. When it comes to structure we should strive for depth.

2. **Durability** How long these structures remain available to us. The more accessible our LTM is, the more useful it is[3]. When it comes to structure we also want durability.

Our job as teachers is to help our students build *deep and durable LTM*, to build enduring understanding (see **Fig. 1**).

But how exactly do we achieve this? To answer that, we need to turn to the other component of our architecture: *Working Memory* (WM).

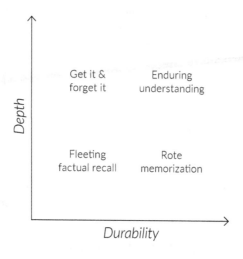

Fig. 1   The dimensions of LTM

Authoring memory

If LTM is our map of the world, then WM is our pencil.

It is the instrument with which we *author* our mental model of reality, the process by which we construct our LTM. It is an instrument that facilitates three interacting processes[4]:

1. **Attention** We select what to focus on for further thinking.
2. **Short term memory** We temporarily hold these foci in our mind.
3. **Elaboration** We attempt to make sense of these objects of focus, drawing on our LTM, and modifying that LTM as a result.

The ways in which our WM executes these processes, within the context of our LTM, determines what we learn. Sometimes this learning is powerful, sometimes not. The more we understand about how this process works, the better we can leverage it in our teaching.

The Matthew Effect

If LTM is equivalent to *knowledge*, then WM is equivalent to *thinking*. The better we think, the more we can know. And the more we know, the better we can think.

This extraordinary relationship between WM and LTM is the reaction engine of education[5]. It is called the *Matthew Effect* and it's our job as teachers to catalyze it[6].

The goal of this book is to help you become a potent catalyst. And the tools we're going to use to help us get there are a set of memory-oriented teaching principles. It's time to unpack this toolbox and see what's inside.

Notes & further reading

1. Memory architecture is much more complex than this, but for the purposes of improving teaching, this model is sufficient

2. LTM appears to be a much more active component than the 'map metaphor' suggests

3. See Bjork's *New theory of disuse* for an overview of the role of access in remembering

4. WM is more likely to be a sub-process of LTM than a separate component itself. See Cowan's *Embedded-processes model of working memory* for more

5. WM capacity is highly correlated with academic ability http://goo.gl/RUOYlx

6. For more, see *The Matthew Effect* by Rigney

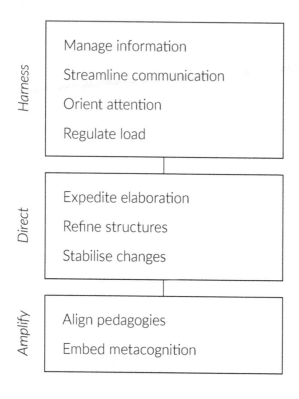

Fig. 2   The 9 principles

The 9 principles

"Memory is the residue of thought."
Willingham

Our goal in teaching is to build powerful LTM. The most direct way we can work towards this goal is by leveraging WM.

Great teachers don't just manage what students *do* in the classroom, they manage what they *think*. Because what students think about is ultimately what they learn.

The following chapters outline a set of actionable principles we can use to help *manage student thinking*. These are the 9 principles of Memorable Teaching (see **Fig. 2**).

Each principle builds on the model of memory established so far, and offers further insights and implications for our practice:

- **Principles 1-4** lay out a set of strategies for *harnessing* WM.
- **Principles 5-7** explore how we can *direct* WM in ways that build powerful LTM.
- **Principles 8-9** outline approaches *amplifying* the impact of the previous principles.

It is important to recognize that the 9 principles are organized around a *simplified model of memory and learning*. The reality of our classrooms is vastly more complex and blurry. However, we need to start somewhere.

The 9 principles provide a framework for thinking differently and more deeply about your practice. They are not a blueprint to be followed, but a starting point for experimentation in context.

Pull on your lab coat and let's dig in.

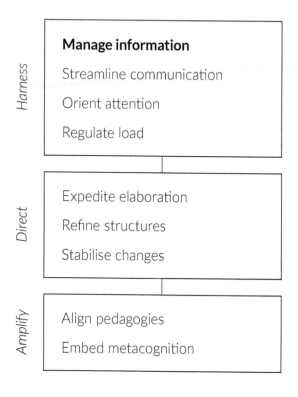

1

Manage information

"There's too much information in the universe. We can only afford to keep the bits that are most likely to prove useful in the future."
Buster[1]

Schools are information rich environments. Our classrooms are overflowing with data.

This information exists in multiple forms. On surfaces covered with text and images. In people's words and behavior. In the routines and culture of our classroom. And all of it *competes for our attention*.

It takes both expertise and energy to filter through this information, to identify what to focus our thinking on next[2]. We are constantly striving to make sense of our environment, so we can gauge where best to *invest* our attention.

Eliminating distractions

From an educational perspective, any information that our students can use to *think closer* to the learning intention is a *desirable*. Everything else is a *distraction*.

It's our job to manage desirables and minimize distractions. Teaching is a zero-sum game. If it's not adding to the learning, it's subtracting from it.

The next time you find yourself in a classroom, ask yourself: *What information is available here? Which aspects are desirable? Which aspects are distractions?*

Of course, we can't get rid of all superfluous information, nor would we want to. But we *can* eliminate a lot. Here are some examples of areas we might want to consider in a cull.

Physical environment

- **Displays** Unless they are being used regularly or in the moment, info-posters or student work on classroom walls can be a distraction[3]. Cover them up, or only bring them out when needed.

- **Clocks** Having a clock in plain view can easily trigger tangential trains of thought. If you are going to have one, (as with display) position it at the back of the room.

- **Music** The only time music helps us think better is when it offsets the impact of other, greater distractions[4]. For example, listening to ambient music using noise cancelling headphones can help people focus in an otherwise noisy environment.

These distractions exist because they offer value in certain contexts. However, we must take care not to justify their place in our classrooms based only on what they *add*. We must also consider what they *subtract* when evaluating the overall value for learning of any information.

Social environment

Social information is particularly tricky to regulate, because it is also the medium through which much learning happens in schools. Nevertheless, small tweaks to classroom routines can add up to big gains in desirable thinking:

- **Interruptions** Crucial explanations and discussions can easily get derailed by a pupil or teacher at the door. Interruptions slow learning and increase mistakes[5]. Build a culture of respect for learning by encouraging visitors to wait for an opportune moment, or to enter only on your signal.

- **Notifications** Smartphone alerts are attention super magnets. Keep them out of sight and mandate that tones and vibrations are disabled. Use dedicated calculators rather than phones where possible.
- **Teachers** Even with the best of intentions, many educators are prone to adversely interfering with student thinking. Minimize classroom narration and other distracting behavior when your students are on task.

Learning tasks and activities

Superfluous information doesn't just exist in the peripheral environment. Learning experiences themselves can be equally distracting.

- **Redundant information** It can be tempting to include superfluous text or images on activity slides and worksheets, or unnecessary words in our explanations. Purge the clipart, keep talk trim.

- **Real life contexts** Situating questions in real-life contexts levies an additional burden on mental processing. Use this only if it helps students make better sense of the material, or is part of the outcome.

- **Unnecessary complexity** Embedding learning in a game or poster may *seem* like an attractive option, but students can end up thinking about game mechanics or pen color at least as much as the topic. Keep it simple. Choose the shortest path[6].

The increasing prevalence of digitally connected tools in our classrooms makes information management more challenging than ever.

Giving students access to the internet while on task is akin to putting 20 televisions on the ceiling and asking them not to look. Just knowing they are there is distraction enough.

Technology can offer great benefits, but the drawbacks are not always obvious. Extra caution is needed when evaluating the costs and benefits of connected tools in the classroom.

Eliminating distractions is a liberating practice. It frees up more time to spend on desirable thinking. Our challenge then becomes: *how do we make the most of the time and information we are left with?* To answer that, we must turn our attention towards streamlining communication.

Notes & further reading

1. From Buster's *Cognitive Bias Cheat Sheet* https://goo.gl/m8hOue

2. Without expertise, we are unable to distinguish between relevant and irrelevant information https://goo.gl/jfM9Ws

3. For more on attention and visual distraction, see https://goo.gl/d9xedB

4. The 'Mozart Effect' is a myth https://goo.gl/SbwRkb

5. Interruptions carry costs both in lag times and error rates https://goo.gl/eBPE5C

6. From *Teach Like a Champion 2.0* by Lemov

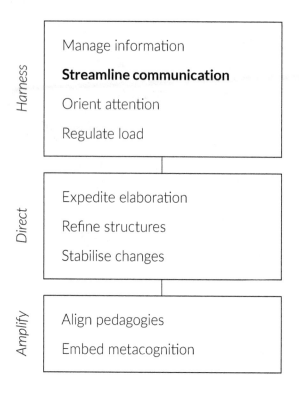

Harness
- Manage information
- **Streamline communication**
- Orient attention
- Regulate load

Direct
- Expedite elaboration
- Refine structures
- Stabilise changes

Amplify
- Align pedagogies
- Embed metacognition

2

Streamline communication

"Wise men speak because they have something to say."
Plato

Teaching is a communication heavy process. Every lesson, *vast amounts of information* move back and forth in a myriad of forms. The way we represent that information (via speech, text, diagrams etc.) and the clarity with which we present it has a big impact on what our students think about.

How we communicate influences *what* gets learned.

Modality

Modality refers to the tools we use to represent information. Things like speech, text, diagrams, images, video and gesture.

Each of these modes has particular advantages and disadvantages. To maximize our impact in the classroom, we need to appreciate these affordances, and draw on them to select the best mode (or combination) for a given situation.

Modes differ in their *linearity, availability* and *flexibility*:

- **Linearity** Text and speech are efficient tools for communicating meaning, particularly abstract concepts. However, they do so in a distinctly linear way. Diagrams can show multiple elements at once, and are better at illustrating how components relate to each other, and fit within an overall context[1].

- **Availability** Speech is ephemeral. It requires students to hold information in their heads whilst listening and trying to make sense of what is being said. Conversely, text and diagrams can be made persistently available, to be processed at the pace of the learner rather than the speaker. If you *are* going to speak for long periods of time, consider building in pauses to allow students to take notes and make sense as you go.

- **Flexibility** Speech is able to relay supplementary information through devices like rhythm and tone. It is also cheaper to produce and easier to adapt than text or diagrams. However, text and diagrams are often more precise, as they can be carefully prepared in advance.

The effectiveness of any signal is determined by how well it is received. Optimizing for modality is about considering the best medium for the message *in the context of what our students know and don't know.*

This should not be confused with selecting modes based on the *learning styles* or *preferences* of our students. We are more similar than different in how we learn, and the labelling of students in this way can be limiting[2].

Get into the habit of asking yourself: *Which parts of my lesson would be best served using speech? Which parts using text or diagrams or video? What role can gesture play[3]?*

Multimodality

Our WM has a particular feature which makes certain combinations of modes particularly potent for learning.

We are able to attend to both speech and diagrams simultaneously, effectively doubling the amount of information we can process at any one time[4]. Crucially, the same does not apply for speech and text.

This is why talking over visuals is one of the most powerful ways to communicate in the classroom. And why reading aloud the notes on your presentation can be counterproductive.

Clarity

Selecting for modality is only part of the streamlining process. We must also seek to increase the *clarity* of our communication[5].

If modality is about *how* information is represented, then clarity is about *how easily* that information can be accessed by our students. This is a function of its *leanness* and *lucidity*.

- **Leanness** How few words or images you use to get your point across.
- **Lucidity** How legible your writing is, or intelligible your speech and drawing is.

To improve the leanness of our communication, we must first get crystal clear about the idea we are trying to convey. Then we can ask: *What is the least I need to say, write or draw for my students to grasp it?*

To increase the lucidity of our communication, we need to get into the habit of looking at our teaching through the eyes of our students, and considering aspects such as:

- **Cadence** The speed at which we speak or show text.
- **Type** The size and style of the fonts we use when displaying text.
- **Contrast** The use of color and light to highlight and connect elements.
- **Labelling** The use of proximity or arrows to connect descriptions with the objects they refer to[6].

There are many ways we could take the study of modality and clarity further, but the most important step is to build an awareness of their place in our practice, so we can be more deliberate in their use.

Notes & further reading

1. Simple diagrams are better than complex ones when learning something new, see *Graphics for Learning* by Clark & Lyons for a comprehensive overview

2. For an in-depth treatment of this issue, see *Stop Propagating the Learning Styles Myth* by Kirschner

3. For more on gesture, see *Visible Learning and the Science of How We Learn* by Hattie (p.140)

4. Also known as *Dual Coding Theory* or the *Modality Effect*

5. For more on the correlation between teacher clarity of communication and student achievement https://goo.gl/F8xLse

6. See *Efficiency in Learning* by Clark *et al*.

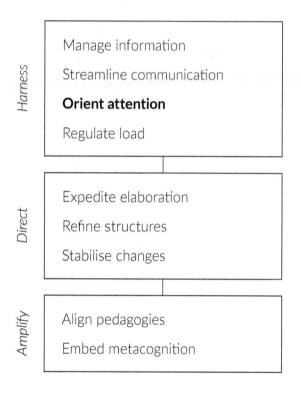

Harness
- Manage information
- Streamline communication
- **Orient attention**
- Regulate load

Direct
- Expedite elaboration
- Refine structures
- Stabilise changes

Amplify
- Align pedagogies
- Embed metacognition

3

Orient attention

"Memory is a crazy old woman that hoards coloured rags and throws away food."
O'Malley

Attention is the process of selecting what to think about next. It is the gatekeeper of our WM, and the ultimate currency of our classrooms.

Our attention has evolved to help us survive and succeed in life[1]. It prioritizes immediate threats and rewards, thrives on the unusual and bizarre, and aggressively filters out anything that doesn't appear to add value.

It is highly idiosyncratic, and not particularly optimized for classroom learning. Left to their own devices, our students may not always focus on the things that will help them make the most progress.

Managing the availability and accessibility of information mitigates this to an extent, but if we really want to increase the predictability of what our students learn, we've also got to actively *orient their attention*.

Precision orientation

We've all seen a £5 (or $5) note hundreds of times, but if I asked you to recreate it, you'd probably struggle. Think about it now, and then check your efforts against **Fig. 3** overleaf.

This is because we tend to filter out many of the visual features of currency, and instead focus what we deem to be *important*. In this case, how much the note is worth.

The amount of information we can attend to in any given moment is severely constrained[2], and where we end up directing that focus on is determined by a messy suite of personal motivations.

If we want to control what our students learn, we've got to be intentional and specific about what they should be attending to. Not only do we need to orient attention, but we must do it with precision.

The set'n'stress approach

Our attention leans on three central mechanisms to help guide it: *filtering*, *following* and *reacting*.

- **Filtering** Sometimes we attend to a thing because that's what we've been looking for or thinking about. When we buy a new red car we notice more red cars on the road.
- **Following** Sometimes we select an object of focus because someone else has directed us towards it. Babies learn to gaze track within their first year[3].

Fig. 3   Filtering out visual noise

- **Reacting** Our attention can also be rapidly re-directed by a *startling stimulus*, like the buzz of a bee or bursting balloon.

Leveraging startling stimuli can be useful when we need to quickly change our student's focus of attention. We can provoke this reaction by clapping hands, blowing whistles or ringing bells.

However, for more precise orientation, leveraging the *filter* and *follow* mechanisms using a simple *set'n'stress* approach will achieve better results.

1. **Set their filter** Explicitly show or tell your students what to look for in advance.
2. **Stress the information** Highlight or emphasize the particular things you've asked them to look for.

Ways we can stress information include:

- **Gesturing** Using our hands, gaze or a pointer to focus attention on particular parts of an image, diagram or text.

- **Accentuating** Pausing or using changes in tone of voice to highlight particular aspects of auditory information.
- **Highlighting** Using italics, bold, underline or color to draw attention to selected portions of a text.

Orienting internally

These strategies are helpful in directing student attention towards particular details in the environment. However, there are also times when we need to direct student attention *inwards*, towards aspects of their own LTM.

This is a slightly more complex challenge, mostly because we're operating in an invisible landscape, but it's one we teachers are well used to navigating.

The simplest way to orient attention inwards is to pose a question. When we're asked *What did you have for breakfast this morning?* our attention immediately orients itself toward the relevant part of our LTM. It's hard *not* to think about it.

Being asked *Why did you have breakfast?* directs your attention to an entirely different area. The questions we ask in the classroom can precisely determine what our students think about.

The strategies outlined in this chapter may seem obvious, but making them a routine part of your practice will not only increase the chances of your students making progress, but can even narrow the attainment gap between them[4].

Notes & further reading

1. Looking at adaptive memory architecture from an evolutionary perspective explains so much https://goo.gl/k9PaES
2. Multi-tasking is a myth – it's really just task switching (which is highly inefficient) and so should be avoided in the classroom where possible
3. For more on the development of gaze tracking, see https://goo.gl/3XtR1R
4. See *Visible Learning and the Science of How We Learn* by Hattie (p.163)

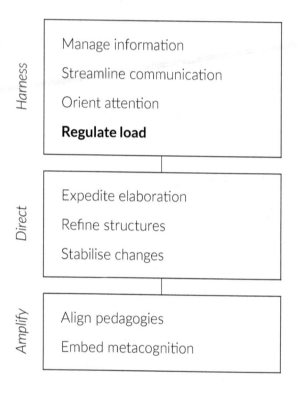

4

Regulate load

"Learning happens when people have to think hard."
Coe

Our WM is a high maintenance mechanism. Give it too little to play with and it begins to look for more interesting fodder. Give it too much to juggle and it'll drop all the balls[1].

This is a delicate balance for teachers to strike, but arguably one of the most significant. Optimizing for impact in the classroom involves not only managing *what* our students are thinking about, but *how hard* we're making them think. We need to regulate cognitive load.

Overload by default

In most situations, our WM is happiest when processing the equivalent of two or three interacting elements at once. Beyond this, its performance begins to rapidly decline[2].

The premise of education makes regulation an intrinsic challenge. We are continually exploring unfamiliar material with our students, and setting them tasks they cannot yet do. The risk of WM overload is persistently present in our practice.

This risk is exacerbated by our own relative familiarity with the material we are teaching. Expert induced blindness makes us prone to underestimating the complexity of tasks and so overestimating the load our students can comfortably bear[3]. It creates an empathy gap that is hard to bridge.

The dice are not stacked in our favor. We are set to overload student thinking by default.

Empathizing with WM load

In your head, attempt to multiply:

- 5 x 5
- 25 x 5
- 75 x 75
- 1111 x 1111

At some point during this sequence, as a result of trying to simultaneously *hold* and *manipulate* multiple pieces of information in your head, most people will begin to struggle.

This is what it feels like to approach (and perhaps exceed) WM overload.

If you had been able to write things down, or knew some nifty multiplication facts, you would have experienced less load. The former reduces the amount of information we need to hold in our heads, and the latter how much manipulating we need to do.

Load factors

The load felt by any student depends not only on the number of interacting elements they are trying to juggle, but on their knowledge of related material, and their familiarity with the contexts in which the learning is taking place.

We can vary the demand felt by WM by adjusting the following *load factors*.

- **Complexity** The number of elements simultaneously being considered, and how they interact.
- **Dependency** To what extent the task draws on prior knowledge or skills.
- **Autonomy** How much we are asking our students to do in their heads.
- **Familiarity** The ease with which students can recognize and navigate the activity or task.

The following pages explore several strategies for regulating load, each of them varying these *load factors* in different ways.

Decomposition

We can reduce the complexity of any task by breaking it down into its constituent components, and giving our students smaller pieces of the puzzle to tackle at a time.

And as they gradually get more familiar with each component, we can increase the number of interacting elements we're asking them to think about at once.

This not only gives students the capability to tackle more challenging material, but can provide crucial injections of motivation through early and repeated success.

Recycling structures

Engaging in tasks with novel structure places an additional burden on student WM. This is load that could be allocated instead towards desirable thinking.

This can be mitigated by recycling familiar task structures and building more routines into our lessons[4].

This approach is particularly powerful for students with low subject self-esteem. Predictability breeds trust, which creates the space to further raise expectations.

Outsourcing

There are times when it is undesirable or impractical to reduce task complexity. In these cases, we can reduce load by *outsourcing* the *short term memory* component of WM.

Outsourcing entails storing live information on *working surfaces*, rather than asking students to hold it in their heads. Ways to do this include:

- **Persistent examples** Leaving model examples or relevant information on the board rather than moving on or wiping it off[5].

- **Capturing thinking** In-class discussions, writing student contributions up on the board as they are given.
- **Offloading information** Encouraging students to pause and write down what they know at each stage of a process.

The more working surfaces in the room, the easier outsourcing becomes. Increase the area available by letting students write on desks, and putting whiteboards on walls[6].

Substituting LTM

The load generated by any task is largely dependent on the relevant prior knowledge of that student. For example, knowing your times-tables inside out means you can devote more of your WM to tackling the higher order aspects of a math(s) question.

However, for various reasons, there are times when our students just don't have the requisite knowledge.

In these cases, we can mitigate overload by temporarily providing *substitute LTM*. Such provision depends on context, but examples include:

- **Thinking tools** Number lines, times tables grids, calculators.
- **Information guides** Fact sheets, writing frames, exemplar models.

It is important to recognize that LTM substitution is a short term strategy. Over time, we must wean our students off such supporting scaffolds, and help them build secure requisite knowledge.

Deep and durable LTM enables our students to tackle tasks with confidence and independence. But more importantly, it reduces the load placed on WM, enabling them to direct mental resources towards the most challenging material.

Effective teaching focuses on building knowledge not only to help our students *think better*, but so they can *learn more* in the future.

These first four chapters have outlined how we might *harness* student thinking. Next, we consider where best to *direct* that thinking, in pursuit of optimal depth and durability.

Notes & further reading

1. This is the basis of Sweller's *Cognitive Load Theory*
2. Miller originally proposed the famous 7+/-2 item limit, but this only holds in the most basic of cases (e.g. random digit recall)
3. See *Visible Learning and the Science of How We Learn* by Hattie (p.12)
4. David Wees is doing some really interesting work in this area with *Instructional Routines* https://goo.gl/iKGhOY
5. The Japanese have a technique called *Bansho* which is a great example of this
6. Carl Hendrick on teaching with floor-to-ceiling whiteboard walls https://goo.gl/tRJ5zn

Harness
- Manage information
- Streamline communication
- Orient attention
- Regulate load

Direct
- **Expedite elaboration**
- Refine structures
- Stabilise changes

Amplify
- Align pedagogies
- Embed metacognition

5

Expedite elaboration

"Science is built up of facts, as a house is with stones. But a collection of facts is no more a science than a heap of stones is a house."
Poincare

Our WM uses our LTM to make sense of the world around us, and in doing so, gradually modifies that LTM.

This process is called *elaboration*, and it provides a useful frame of reference to guide us in directing student thinking.

Elaboration explains why student learning is *limited by what they know*, why it is crucial to *start where our students are at*, and advance their understanding *one small step at a time*. It explains why *knowing what our students know* is one of the best investments a teacher can make.

In the rest of this chapter, we're going to explore two teaching techniques we can lean on to expedite elaboration: *priming* and *tethering*.

Priming

What we are able to learn is limited by what we know. Or perhaps more accurately: how easily we can *access* that relevant knowledge.

We can increase the chances of learning happening by activating, or *warming up* relevant areas of LTM before exploring a new topic. This is called *priming*.

Priming for learning is a bit like priming for painting. We prepare the surface to help our material stick better. Ways to prime LTM include:

- **Pre-review** Revisiting requisite knowledge prior to elaboration. Don't make the material challenging. The goal here is simply to reactivate relevant knowledge[1].
- **Advance organization** Outlining the broader structural composition of a new concept or topic in advance.

Pre-review is an established practice in many classrooms. It happens when we give our students a quiz, offer recaps, or simply ask them to free-recall what they know about a particular thing, often in the early phases of a lesson.

Advance organization is a slightly less common practice. Techniques we might use include:

- **Bigger picturing** Establishing where the forthcoming learning *fits* within the broader structure of a topic or subject.

- **Knowledge pre-organization** Providing students with an organized overview of all the knowledge they are going to learn in a topic[2].

- **Relevance structuring** Exploring *why* we're learning these things.

- **Similar skeletons** Connecting the intended learning to previous content that has a similar meta-structure. For example, before exploring *the relationship between the area of a circle and its circumference,* revisiting how *the area of a rectangle relates to its perimeter.*

Tethering

If priming is about establishing effective *pre-conditions* for new learning, then tethering is about giving that learning the best possible start.

It involves anchoring new insights to existing ones. This not only makes those insights easier to grasp, but increases their initial connectedness.

Here are some ways we can tether new ideas:

- **Inference** Bringing together existing ideas in logical ways to create new insights. For example, the area of a triangle can be *inferred* by combining an understanding of *the area of a rectangle* with that of *the relationship between a triangle and a rectangle.*

- **Analogy** Using a concept our students are familiar with as the starting point for scaffolding a new mental model. For example, using a set of weighing scales to help students start to build an understanding of the role of *balancing the sides* in solving equations.

- **Concrete bridging** Providing students with concepts in their most tangible form, and then using these as a basis for representing them in increasingly abstract ways. For example, exploring the volume of a cube (ideally providing your students with a physical cube) before learning what x^3 means.

Tethering can be a powerful approach in helping students make rapid progress in the early stages of understanding. However, it can also be a hindrance if not deployed carefully.

For example, analogy (by definition) is only an approximation of the concept it is being used to seed. Once students have achieved basic and secure understanding, it is important to highlight the limitations of any founding analogy.

Similarly, concrete forms can limit the development of abstract understanding (and even overload WM) if not withdrawn at a suitable point[3].

Mnemonics

Tethering doesn't lend itself to every situation. Certain concepts just don't offer that many meaningful connections to what students already know. As a result, we need a different approach to help students remember these *isolated ideas*.

One way we can do this is to *fabricate* connections around such concepts. The resulting artificial structures are known as *mnemonics*.

Here are some ways mnemonics can be used[5]:

- **Rhyme** Embedding isolated information in songs or poems can make it easier to recall. The more rhythmic, unusual or annoying the better.

- **Letter linking** Using various word-letter relationships as cues, e.g. *GEMS* or *BIDMAS* as acrostics to recall the order of mathematical operations, or *I Value Xylophones Like Cows Dig Milk* for roman numeral symbols. This can even be used to remember number strings, e.g. Word lengths in *How I wish I could calculate pi* for 3.141592

- **Stories** Our minds are particularly well suited to processing information in narrative form. We find stories easier to comprehend and remember[6].

Mnemonics can be helpful in increasing the *durability* of LTM, but their lack of meaningful connections makes them less useful for building *depth* in understanding. Mnemonics are best seen as an *addition to*, rather than *replacement for* more elaborative approaches.

Notes & further reading

1. Bodil Isaksen on the need for a *Nothing New, Just Review* section in lessons https://goo.gl/VsDJkF
2. For more see *Knowledge Organisers* by Kirby https://goo.gl/Vmygm3
3. For a nuanced analysis of the influence of manipulatives, see https://goo.gl/ooOoVK
4. In *Visible Learning and the Science of How We Learn* Hattie suggests that only 20% of non-connected learning can be recalled a day later (p.116)
5. For more mnemonics, see *Visible Learning and the Science of How We Learn* by Hattie (p.171) and *Why Don't Students Like School?* by Willingham (p.77)
6. For more, see *The Privileged Status of Story* by Willingham https://goo.gl/lTej1f

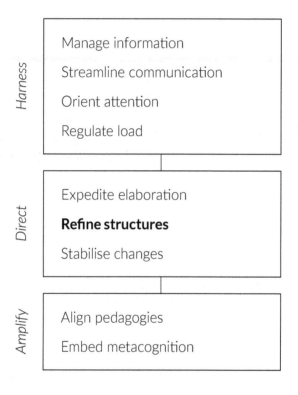

6

Refine structures

"Understanding is not a miraculous threshold that we cross once. It is a gradual, liminal accumulation and reordering of knowledge."
Ashman[1]

Like building a physical structure, building understanding is not something that happens instantaneously. It is something that must be constructed bit by bit, one piece at a time.

Unlike construction, we do not always have intricate plans to work from. Instead, we must establish a vision for the architecture of our understanding by feeling out similar structures with our eyes closed.

When we first encounter a new concept, it is not always obvious where that concept ends and its context begins. As a result, aspects of context often get encoded in our LTM alongside aspects of concept.

This is part of the reason students struggle to transfer concepts to different domains, and why students find it hard to do math(s) in a science lab.

The process of elaboration is idiosyncratic, gradual and iterative. In the early stages of learning, LTM will often be:

- **Blurry** Only partially formed and not clearly distinct from similar concepts.
- **Simple** Basic in structure, with superficial connections to related concepts.
- **Shallow** Tied tightly to particular contexts and not easily applied to different situations.

Grasping new ideas is only a small part of the learning process. It is the *refinement* of those ideas that brings depth and power to student learning.

Our job as teachers is not only to seed new insights, but to help our students make sense of and iterate them. To meld them into abstract and complex mental models that can be wielded with confidence and independence[2].

Two strategies we can use to refine LTM in the classroom are *variation* and *definition*.

Variation

What we think about is what we learn. Yet our thinking is limited by what we can perceive. When something is perceived, it gets separated or *abstracted* from its context. It becomes less blurry and shallow in our minds.

We can refine student LTM by drawing their attention towards, and helping them see or *discern*, the defining aspects of an idea.

We can do this by presenting students with a *contrasting range* of examples and experiences, between which certain aspects change and others remain the same.

This is called *variation*, and not only helps separate concepts from their contexts, but gives them greater transferrable punch[3]. Variation builds both abstraction *and* generalization. This is what makes it such a potent tool in the pursuit of deep LTM.

Variation in action

For example, if we wanted to help someone refine their understanding of what a triangle is, we might begin by establishing the *defining* and the relevant *non-defining* aspects of the concept:

- **Defining aspects** 3-sides, straight sides, closed shape.
- **Relevant non-defining aspects** Length of sides, similarity of angles, orientation.

We'd then present students with a range of *examples* and *non-examples* (shapes that are *not* triangles) to draw attention to these particular aspects and illustrate *just how much a shape can change* while continuing to remain a triangle (see **Fig. 4**).

The presentation of non-examples is an important part of this process. It enables us to establish and refine the boundaries of a concept. In variation, *difference* is as important as *similarity*.

Perceiving differences can be hard, especially when it comes to the subtler variations required for more refined understanding. Where possible, make it easier for your students to *spot the difference* by presenting examples side-by-side.

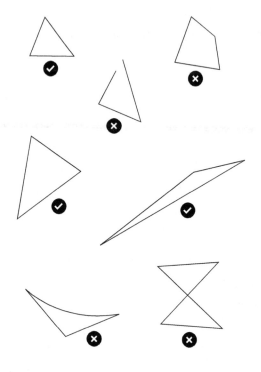

Fig. 4   Conceptual variation

Variations on variation

The triangle example outlined here illustrates just one of several ways to leverage variation. Depending on the subject being studied, alongside our learning intentions, approaches we might consider include:

- **Conceptual variation** Presenting examples and non-examples to refine the understanding of a particular concept (as illustrated in **Fig. 4**).

- **Relational variation** Illustrating how changing one variable impacts another, to refine a causal or correlated connection.

- **Situational variation** Providing a broad range of application problems, in pursuit of a more integrated and generalized understanding of the concept.

- **Contextual variation** Experiencing the concept or its application in different guises or environments, to develop increasingly abstract understanding[4].

It is important to remember that variation is about drawing attention to granular aspects of an idea. This can only happen if we keep our changes minimal. Variation quickly loses utility if we change too many things at once.

Separating similar concepts

When we first encode a new concept, it can often not only get mixed up with its immediate context[5], but also any *similar* concepts being explored during that lesson.

For example, if we introduce the concepts of *area* and *perimeter* close together in our teaching, it is likely that the cues for each of these concepts will overlap in student LTM structures.

When asked to explain how to find the area of a rectangle, students taught in this way often say something like: *you multiply or add the sides, but I can't remember which.*

Help your students develop clearer and more distinct understanding around the identities and meanings of concepts by separating them from similar concepts at the point of introduction[6].

Once this has been achieved we can further strengthen that understanding by pulling these similar concepts together, highlighting their differences and exploring their relationships.

Iterating towards definition

Variation can be a powerful tool for giving a concept meaning. However, it cannot always capture that meaning in a precise or easily portable way.

To achieve this, we need to spend time thinking about how to *codify* that concept in a concise and comprehensive form[7]. About how we might describe and organise it, while considering how it relates to similar concepts, and fits within an overall subject domain.

This is called *definition*, and ways to do it include:

- **Articulation** Activities that encourage students to describe a concept or process precisely. E.g. summaries, alien explanation[8], peer teaching.
- **Reorganization** Activities that help students discriminate a concept from similar concepts. E.g. Venn diagrams, similarity/difference identification, categorization/classification.

Used in tandem, variation and definition can generate heavily connected and refined LTM. Understanding that is both rich in meaning and economical in structure.

This kind of deep LTM puts our students in a strong position, but it is insufficient by itself. In the next chapter we turn our attention to the other component needed for powerful LTM: *durability*.

Notes & further reading

1. From *Six Tips to Improve your Explicit Teaching* https://goo.gl/8QIHsf
2. For more on high structure vs low structure learners see *Make It Stick* by Brown *et al.* (p.153)
3. For more, see *Variation Theory and the Improvement of Teaching and Learning* by Lo
4. For more on the power of representing ideas in multiple ways https://goo.gl/ooOoVK
5. For a strong discussion on the problems of context, see *Transfer of Learning* by Cristina Milos https://goo.gl/EdLfJV
6. Bruno Reddy on the *Separation of Minimally Difference Concepts* https://goo.gl/I4f8h9
7. On *Learning Concepts from Definitions* by Anderson & Kulhavy (£)
8. Explaining a concept to a peer as if they are an alien

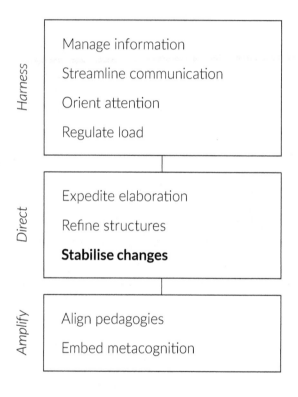

7

Stabilize changes

*"Civilization advances by extending the number of
important operations we can perform without thinking
about them."*
Whitehead

Building deep LTM is a worthy investment. It helps
our students to understand the world and solve the
problems they encounter. And most importantly, it
enables them to *learn more*.

However, deep LTM is only useful if we can access
it. Building depth is a waste of time if we don't also
invest in making that LTM easily and continually
available. Understanding relies on remembering.
Depth requires durability.

The problem is that our minds have evolved to be highly efficient information processors, only keeping those things they deem most important.

As a result, our memories are programmed to decay by default, from the moment they are formed[1]. This process is exacerbated when we try to learn other things at the same time[2]. Schooling sets itself a tough challenge.

As teachers, we must start with the assumption that our students will forget what they have learned *unless we take deliberate steps to help them remember.* What kinds of steps might these be?

Retrieval vs re-exposure

Every time we draw on a memory, we increase its strength and extend its longevity. This is called *retrieval*, and it is the primary process by which we build durability in LTM[3].

The less assistance we provide students during retrieval, the greater the strengthening effect. This is why posing your students questions about a topic is more powerful than presenting that topic again. *Retrieval beats re-exposure.*

We can further optimize retrieval effects by posing questions that are:

- **Answerable** Retrieval is about remembering things you already know, not about scaffolding new insights.

- **Unhelpful** Questions should provide minimal clues to the answer. This is why multiple-choice questions aren't ideal for inducing retrieval.

- **Low stakes** If students perceive the consequences of a test to be too high, anxiety can interfere with the effects of retrieval. Reinforce this by not awarding grades and using terms like 'quiz'.

- **Self-serving** Exploit the hyper-correction effect by getting student to mark and correct their own answers[4].

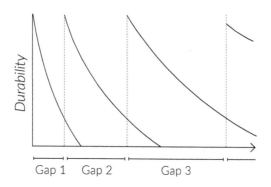

Fig. 5   Optimal retrieval spacing[5]

Spaced retrieval

Durability is generated not only as a result of *what* we direct our students to think about, but *when* that thinking occurs.

The most beneficial time for someone to retrieve a memory is just before they forget it. Combine this timing with the resulting strengthening effect of retrieval, and we end up with a pattern of increasingly distributed intervals between quizzes or questions (see **Fig. 5**).

This is called *spacing* and is one of the quickest wins available for teachers wishing to supercharge their impact.

The optimal spacing for each student depends on a swathe of complex factors[6]. Aiming for precision in scheduling can quickly become cripplingly complicated, and so a more pragmatic bet is just to build regular *cumulative quizzes* into your teaching.

These are loose compositions of questions drawn from topics covered anytime from last week to six months ago.

Interleaving

Spacing is about inducing retrieval *between* lessons, but these effects can also be exploited *within* a lesson.

We can achieve this by simply getting our students to think about something else for a while, creating the opportunity to induce retrieval again.

This is called *interleaving*, and an easy way to apply it is to make every third or fourth question in a problem set based on a previous topic[7].

As an added bonus, this enhances durability for the other topic too. Spacing and interleaving are mutually reinforcing.

Automacy

The amount of retrieval practice students need depends on the degree of durability we wish to create.

Three or four well-spaced retrievals are often sufficient to generate a fairly long-lasting memory. This provides a strong platform for problem solving and further learning, and so for many situations, is a satisfactory outcome.

However, in certain cases we want to build more than just endurance. Sometimes we want to foster remembering that is also rapid and effortless. Access that is *automatic*.

Automacy is the mechanism that enables us to perform the myriad complex actions required to drive, whilst also listening to the radio or talking with fellow passengers.

It is the mechanism that allows us to decode multiple words in succession during reading, and simultaneously focus on the meaning of a passage.

The more automatic our memories, the less load they place on our WM. The less load on our WM, the more capacity we can devote to new learning.

Automacy is an incredibly powerful state of durability, but it takes significant amounts of retrieval practice to attain. It is an investment best kept for the *highest leverage* content of a subject[8].

Delayed returns

One of the most challenging aspects of implementing the principles outlined in this and the previous chapter is that although they enhance learning in the long run, they don't always *feel* productive in the short term.

For example, when we space or vary our practice, we may find that our students make more errors and slower progress[9]. It would be easy to conclude that these strategies are ineffective, and resort to more familiar forms of practice.

However, this would neglect how blocked practice (in contrast with spaced or varied forms) allows our students to lean upon both the context of the lesson, as well as the structure of previous problems, to help them answer questions and respond to tasks.

It is a kind of invisible scaffold which, if we're not careful, can lead us to confusing what our students can *do* with what they have *learned*. That is not to say that assessment during a lesson is worthless. Just that we need to be careful about the conclusions we draw from it.

These last few chapters have explored how we can *direct* thinking in ways that build depth and durability. Now, we turn our attention to two approaches that can *amplify* the impact of our practice.

Notes & further reading

1. It appears to be our *access* to those memories which decays, rather than the memories themselves https://goo.gl/WucsPJ
2. On retroactive interference https://goo.gl/xbR1om
3. For more on how retrieval interrupts forgetting, see *Make It Stick* by Brown *et al.* (p.20)
4. From Craig Barton's *Podcast with Dylan Wiliam* https://goo.gl/2qsMqT
5. Based on the *Ebbinghaus Forgetting Curve*
6. For example, the Learning Scientists explain how sleep can consolidate memory https://goo.gl/jgNRCS
7. From *Recent Research on Human Learning Challenges Conventional Instructional Strategies* by Rohrer & Pashler (£)
8. This is why numeracy and literacy have such prominent profiles within schools
9. From *Recent Research on Human Learning Challenges Conventional Instructional Strategies* by Rohrer & Pashler (£)

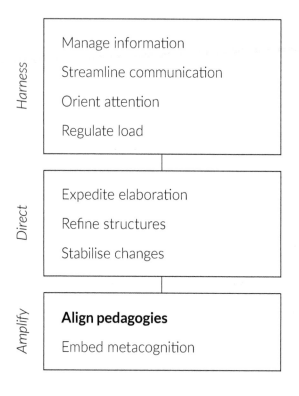

8

Align pedagogies

"Speak clearly, if you speak at all. Carve every word before you let it fall."
Holmes

Constructing understanding is a multi-layered activity. As with building a physical structure, it moves back and forth through various phases: erecting overarching skeleta; assembling sub-components; fitting the pieces together; and integrating with local infrastructure.

And just like the physical build process, different phases of learning demand different tools.

Part of effective teaching is selecting the right tool for the job. A misaligned pedagogical approach will falter no matter how well it is executed. We can't use a hammer to tighten a bolt (we'd probably destroy the bolt if we tried).

To select the right pedagogical tool for the job, we need to understand the various possibilities or *affordances* that the approaches available offer our students[1].

Let's explore this idea further by examining some ubiquitous teacher tools (presentation and practice), why we might select them, and how we can wield them to greatest effect.

Presentation vs practice

In the early stages of learning, we strive to erect a loose skeletal framework upon which subsequent insights can be hung. The composition of this initial framework determines how easily we can transition towards more comprehensive and complex understanding.

Establishing a helpful initial skeleton is hard to do without guidance, because we don't know what we don't know. A more efficient and reliable approach is to copy an existing one. This is why *teacher presentation* is an effective tool in the early stages of understanding.

However, the incremental nature of elaboration limits our ability to replicate anything too complex to begin with. At this stage, a simplified, *bare-bones* framework has greatest utility (one of the reasons *analogy* is such a potent teaching tool).

Crafting and presenting *bare-bones* frameworks is not as easy as it might first appear. As (relative) subject experts, our understanding is inherently complex, and often quite tacit.

The best presentation simplifies complexity to a level that makes sense to our students, teases out the essential from the non-essential, and makes the implicit explicit[2].

With a loose skeleton is in place, we can fruitfully begin to attend to structure at a more granular level. When it comes to filling in the details, and integrating fresh insights with existing LTM, *student practice* is a more appropriate approach.

The best practice is not fancy or complicated. It exposes our students to a carefully sequenced set of experiences, in pursuit of precise developments in understanding, while providing timely, *course-correcting* feedback along the way[3].

The more basic the practice activity, the more attention we can direct toward the details, enabling us to teach in a *highly intentional way*.

Transitions & cycles

Presentation and practice can be powerful pedagogical tools for particular stages of learning. However, our students don't just jump neatly from one stage to the next.

If we want to keep our teaching aligned with the needs of our students, we need to offer a *faded transition* experience between presentation and practice. Examples of ways to do this include:

- **Me-we-you** We model an example, then use student questioning to guide us in completing a similar example, before letting them try some on their own. A time-honored classic.

- **Completion examples** We provide students with a suite of *increasingly incomplete* examples to guide them incrementally towards independence[4].

The *idiosyncratic* nature of learning means that these transitions are likely to be more jagged than smooth, as our students make progress in fits and starts.

The *incremental* nature of learning means that our cycles of presentation-practice are best kept tight. Long cycles can overload student WM, leaving their focus depleted and attention wandering[5].

Means-ends conflation

One of the core aims of education is to create people capable of critically analyzing and solving a diverse range of problems within a specialist domain.

However, we must be careful about conflating our ends with our means. Giving someone problems to solve is not always the best way to make them an effective problem solver, particularly for students at the early stages of understanding[6]. As Crehan so eloquently observes:

> "We teach problem solving through math(s), not math(s) through problem solving. We teach critical thinking through history, not history through critical thinking.[7]"

Without sufficient understanding to steer thinking, inquiry-based approaches can quickly overload WM, frustrate our students, and generate idiosyncratic understanding and misconceptions[8].

Notes & further reading

1. For more, see Gibson's *Theory of Affordances*
2. When we make logical leaps in our teaching, our students must create their own logic to fill those gaps, argues Wees in *Making Mathematical Ideas Explicit* https://goo.gl/wO3TSu
3. For more on the complexities and challenges of timing feedback for optimal learning, see *Make It Stick* by Brown *et al.* (p.40)
4. For more on the completion examples, see *Efficiency in Learning* by Clark *et al.*
5. From *Visible Learning and the Science of How We Learn* by Hattie (p.48)
6. For a rigorous and cogent discussion on this counter-intuitive issue see *Making Good Progress* by Christodoulou
7. From the wonderful *Cleverlands* by Crehan
8. For more, see *Why Don't Students Like School?* by Willingham

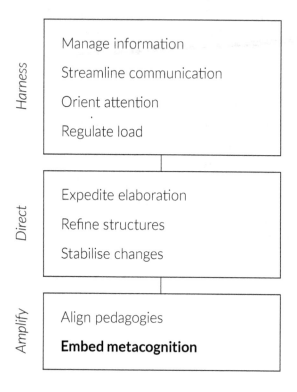

Harness
- Manage information
- Streamline communication
- Orient attention
- Regulate load

Direct
- Expedite elaboration
- Refine structures
- Stabilise changes

Amplify
- Align pedagogies
- **Embed metacognition**

9

Embed metacognition

"What is necessary to change a person is to change his awareness of himself."
Maslow

Our impact as teachers may be significant, but it is severely limited by how our students approach their learning[1]. We can extend our reach of influence by enabling our students to learn memorably even when we're not directly managing their attention[2].

The practice of *thinking about thinking* is called *metacognition*, and in a classroom context, can benefit from the following three components:

1. **Meta-knowledge** Students develop an understanding of memorable learning principles and strategies.
2. **Self-regulation** Students are clear about their academic goals, aware of how they are progressing towards them, and can *course-correct* in the moment.
3. **Calibration** Students are able to *accurately* assess their own level of understanding.

Building meta-knowledge is no different to learning about any other concept. The principles in this book can be taught using the principles in this book.

We can support this process by routinely outlining the rationale underpinning our teaching approaches. This not only builds metacognition but increases *buy-in*, as students grow to appreciate why they are doing what they are doing.

In general, the more we expose and demystify the learning process, the more agency our students will come to have over it.

Self-regulation

The second aspect of metacognition is self-regulation. This is about monitoring our thinking and action, and modifying our approach should we start to drift off course.

Effective self-regulation requires not only *goal clarity*, but *self-awareness*. We need to catch ourselves thinking or doing something before we can change it.

Building attentional awareness is a relatively underdeveloped practice in education[3]. However, *check-ins* offer an interesting starting point for experimentation:

- **Trigger** Set an alarm to go off at 15-minute-or-so intervals during your lessons.

- **Check-in** Following the trigger, students make a quick note of what they have been thinking about, and then get straight back to what they were doing.

It can take time for the muscle-like capability of self-awareness to develop, but when it does, your students will start to notice more of what they are attending to, and (assuming they are clear on their goals) begin to auto-self-correct.

Over time, your students will spend more time thinking desirably, and less time distracted. But perhaps most importantly, they will end up with a greater sense of agency over their thoughts and actions.

Calibration

Student regulation of thinking is important, but for metacognition to function fully, our students also need to be able to accurately assess their own understanding, to determine what they know and don't know at any given time.

This is not something we are naturally good at. Left to our own devices we tend to overestimate what we know, and underestimate how long it will take us learn something[4].

We can mitigate this by providing regular opportunities for our students to *calibrate* their understanding. Here's one way to do this:

1. **Predict** Get your student to anticipate how they will score on a question, quiz or test *before* they attempt it.
2. **Evaluate** Afterwards, help them determine their performance, using an objective and unambiguous assessment framework.
3. **Reflect** Provide space for them to notice any differences between their initial prediction and final score, and to reflect on how they might judge more accurately next time[5].

Gradual introduction

There are two things to be aware of when embedding metacognition.

The first is that *thinking about thinking* consumes WM capacity. Monitoring attention demands attention, and check-ins disrupt thinking.

These initial distractions will eventually pay off, but it is still best to introduce them gradually and integrate them sparingly.

The other factor we must consider is the *self-talk of self-regulation*. The narrative our students adopt when monitoring their own thinking can inhibit progress if it generates too much of an emotional response[6]. Self-talk oriented around observation beats self-talk oriented around judgement.

We can support our students with this by creating an environment, and building routines that encourage them to ask: *What am I thinking?* and *How could I think differently?* rather than *Am I doing well enough?* or *Why can't I do this?*

Finally, the context-dependent nature of learning means that these strategies will find most traction when *baked in* to our everyday classroom activities, rather than *bolted on* in the form of standalone 'metacognition lessons'.

Notes & further reading

1. Hattie estimates student influences at 50%, compared with teacher influences at 30% https://goo.gl/QdcgYE
2. For more, see the EEF's *Metacognition Toolkit*
3. There are some interesting overlaps in research on mindfulness, see *Mindfulness* by Williams & Penman (p.50)
4. In *Why Don't Students Like School?* Willingham suggests that, left to their own devices, students will typically only study two-thirds of the amount required to achieve comprehensive learning
5. In *Make It Stick*, Brown *et al.* argue that good judgement must be learnt (p.104)
6. For more, see *The Effort Effect* by Krakovsky https://goo.gl/hMfnJV

Long-term teaching

"Are things getting better or worse? In the short term the pessimists are right, and in the long term the optimists are right."
Saffo

Memorable teaching is a plain, restrained approach to building learning. It relies on simple routines executed with frequency, and is predicated on the idea that learning, and teaching, *takes time*.

For memorable principles to bear fruit, we need to view our practice through a *long-term lens*.

This is no easy task. Long-term teaching demands patience, trust and a certain strength of character. We work in a landscape of ever increasing performativity, where we are asked to do more, and with more urgency, than ever before.

If we're not careful, these conditions can drive our decisions, and limit our impact. Instead, we must be prepared to invest in, and defend those practices which offer the greatest returns for our students over time. We must be willing to play the long game.

Thank you for taking the time to read this book, and for making yourself a more impactful teacher. This is one of the greatest long-term investments you can make.

Thank yous

> *"Never doubt that a small group of thoughtful, committed citizens can change the world. Indeed, it is the only thing that ever has."*
> Mead

Book writing doesn't happen in a vacuum. I am massively grateful to everyone who helped make Memorable Teaching happen:

- To Mike and Karlos for their bottomless pub-philosophy appetite
- To Mum, Dad, Em and Laura for their unwavering enthusiasm & support
- To Kris Boulton, Graeme Robertson, Joe LM, Matt Benyohai, Richard Russell, Mo Ladak & Philip Jones for their eagle eyes
- To everyone at the IfT for opening my eyes to a whole different league of ambition for educational improvement
- And to all you bloggers out there relentlessly searching for the truth

EXPERT
TEACHING

Peps Mccrea

LEAN
LESSON
PLANNING

Peps Mccrea

MOTIVATED TEACHING

Peps Mccrea